Toilet Paper

BEFORE THE STORE

BY RACHEL LYNETTE • ILLUSTRATED BY DAN McGEEHAN

Published by The Child's World®
1980 Lookout Drive • Mankato, MN 56003-1705
800-599-READ • www.childsworld.com

ACKNOWLEDGMENTS
The Child's World®: Mary Berendes, Publishing Director
The Design Lab: Design and production
Red Line Editorial: Editorial direction
Content Consultant: S. Jack Hu, Ph.D., J. Reid and Polly Anderson Professor of Manufacturing
Technology, Professor of Mechanical Engineering and Industrial and Operations Engineering,
The University of Michigan

ISBN 9781609736835
LCCN 2011940079

PHOTO CREDITS
Mersant/Dreamstime, cover, 1, back cover; Nick Stubbs/Dreamstime, cover (inset); 1 (inset); Olga
Miltsova/Bigstock, 5; Kitch Bain/Shutterstock Images, 7; Krokodils/Fotolia, 9; Dave Willman/Bigstock,
11, 30; iStockphoto, 15; LVV/Shutterstock Images, 18; Kybele/Fotolia, 21, 31 (top); Jiri Hera/Shutterstock
Images, 24; Eugene Tochilin/Bigstock, 27, 31 (bottom left); Viorel Dudau/Dreamstime, 29, 31 (bottom right)

Design elements: Mersant/Dreamstime

Printed in the United States of America

ABOUT THE AUTHOR

Rachel Lynette has written more than 100 books for children as well as many teacher resources. In addition, she writes blogs for teachers. Rachel lives near Seattle, Washington. She has a daughter in high school and a son in college.

Contents

CHAPTER ONE

Useful Toilet Paper

Toilet paper is something most people do not think about. But, when you run out of toilet paper, it becomes really important. Many people have a favorite type of toilet paper. Some people choose recycled toilet paper. And others choose extra thick toilet paper. You can buy it in small and big rolls, too.

Have you ever thought about how toilet paper is made? There are many steps. For recycled toilet paper, the first step starts with old paper. However, most toilet paper starts at a tree farm or forest. That is where trees are cut.

In our bathrooms, toilet paper is important.

CHAPTER TWO

Tree Fibers

The wood in trees has tiny **fiber** strands. Some fiber is short and some is long. The fibers are stuck together by natural glue. It is called **lignin**. To make paper, the fibers are pulled apart. The lignin is removed. Then the fibers are put together again.

Toilet paper is made from both hardwood and softwood trees. Hardwood trees include maple, oak, and eucalyptus. They grow where the weather is warm. Spruce, pine, and Douglas fir are softwood trees. They grow where the weather is colder. Both types of wood

Most toilet paper is made from 70 percent hardwood and 30 percent softwood.

make toilet paper both soft and strong. It must be soft so it is comfortable to use. It must be strong so that it does not fall apart.

Eucalyptus trees are a type of hardwood tree.

CHAPTER THREE

From Logs to Pulp

Toilet paper companies grow many of the trees they need on large tree farms. The rest of the trees come from natural forests. Many different animals live in the forests. The trees make oxygen for the planet. Trees are **renewable** resources. When trees are cut down, new trees can be planted. However, trees take a long time to grow. And animals lose their homes when trees are cut. That is why many people think it is better to use recycled paper in toilet paper.

Trees are cut using large machines or chainsaws.

Millions of trees are cut to make toilet paper every year. Often large machines are used to cut the trees. Trees are also cut down with chainsaws. Next the branches are removed with a machine. Then the logs are put on large trucks and taken to the paper factory.

At the paper factory, machines strip the bark away from the wood. Then a machine with spinning blades cuts the logs into small chips. About 50 tons (45 tonnes) of wood chips are mixed with 10,000 gallons (37,854 L) of **chemicals**. This mix is cooked

A machine removes the bark from the log.

in a machine called a digester for three hours. The chemicals and the heat separate the fibers. Much of the water **evaporates** from the wood.

The chips change in the digester. They turn into a thick paste called **pulp**. The pulp weighs less than wood chips. It now weighs just 25 tons (22 tonnes). The lignin is still in the pulp. But it no longer holds the fibers together.

Next the pulp is washed to take out the lignin and chemicals. Toilet paper turns yellow if it still has lignin. The lignin that is removed is used as fuel to help run the factory.

The chips are boiled into pulp in a machine.

CHAPTER FOUR

Recycled Paper

Most toilet paper is still made from trees, but some is made from recycled paper. Junk mail, magazines, and newspapers can be recycled. This paper is dumped into a large tank called a pulper. A pulper is kind of like a giant washing machine. It mixes all of the paper with warm water for about ten minutes. This turns it into pulp. The pulper is also a **filter**. It takes out staples, paperclips, and other bits of metal and plastic.

Recycled toilet paper saves trees. It also keeps more garbage from going into garbage dumps.

Old pieces of paper become recycled toilet paper.

Next the ink is removed from the pulp. In a machine, air is pushed into the pulp. The ink sticks to the air bubbles. The air bubbles rise to the top of the mix. Then the bubbly foam is taken off the top by the machine. The pulp below does not have any ink. But, the pulp is still not white. It is a light-brown color. It has to be **bleached** to make it white.

At this point, the pulp is still wet. The paper cannot be bleached while it is wet. The pulp moves through several large rollers. They squeeze out the water in the pulp. Now the pulp can **absorb** the chemicals that make it white.

Ink sticks to air bubbles in the pulp.

CHAPTER FIVE

From Pulp to Paper

The next steps are the same for pulp from trees or recycled paper. The pulp is first bleached. Bleaching takes out the color and makes the pulp white. The pulp is treated with chemicals.

Not all toilet paper is bleached. If you have used toilet paper that is

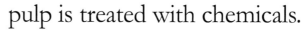

Recycled toilet paper can be light-brown in color.

light-brown, it has probably not been bleached. Often recycled toilet paper is not bleached.

Next the pulp is mixed with water. This makes a liquid called paper stock. The paper stock has 99.5 percent water and only .5 percent pulp. The paper stock is sprayed onto a large and wide moving screen. The screen lets most of the water drain away. A thin film

Paper stock dries on a screen.

of pulp is left. The water that drains off is cleaned in machines. Then it is used again in the factory. Next the screen goes over rollers. The rollers press the paper and take out more water. The pulp enters a machine called the Yankee Dryer. The dryer quickly dries the pulp into very thin paper.

Metal blades scrape the paper off the Yankee Dryer. This causes it to **crepe**. The paper now has tiny wrinkles. This makes it feel softer. The paper is then wound onto a long and wide spool. It makes a giant roll of paper. These rolls are very big! They can weigh as much as 5 tons (4 tonnes).

A single giant roll
has nearly 47 miles
(76 km) of paper!

The paper is rolled onto a giant spool.

CHAPTER SIX

Patterns and Sheets

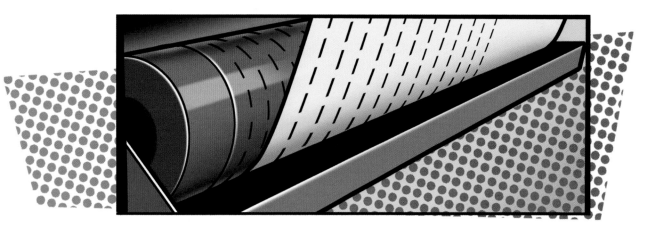

The paper does not stay on the giant spool for very long. A forklift moves and loads the spool onto a

A machine puts a pattern onto the toilet paper.

converting machine. The converting machine unwinds the paper. Then two things happen to the paper.

Have you seen the tiny pattern on most kinds of toilet paper? To make that pattern, the paper goes over a special roller. The roller is covered with raised bumps. When the paper rolls over it, the pattern presses into the paper. The toilet paper is now **embossed**.

Next the paper must be **perforated**. This makes sheets that tear easily and evenly. The perforation roller has rows of pins. When the paper rolls over it, the pins make a row of tiny holes across the paper.

For most brands, a row of perforation holes appears every 4.5 inches (11.5 cm).

The toilet paper moves onto the winding machine. The paper is glued to and wound onto long cardboard tubes. When the roll is full, a machine cuts the paper. Then a new roll is started. The machine also glues the end of the toilet paper to the roll. This stops the paper from coming off the tube.

Once it is perforated, a sheet from a roll of toilet paper is easy to rip off.

The average American uses 57 sheets of toilet paper every day. That is 20,805 sheets a year!

Next the tubes are cut to the correct size. They move into a machine with a circular saw. It cuts each long roll into many smaller rolls. Now the rolls are finished. They are ready to be put into packages.

The long spools are cut into rolls.

CHAPTER SEVEN

Wrapping the Rolls

The toilet paper moves on a **conveyor belt** to the packaging area. Most toilet paper is wrapped in plastic. It is sold in packages of four to 30 rolls. Machines wrap the rolls in plastic. The label is printed on the plastic before it goes over the rolls. Some rolls are wrapped in paper. The toilet paper is stored in warehouses. The rolls are ready to be shipped by trains and trucks to stores.

Most toilet paper is wrapped in packs with plastic.

CHAPTER EIGHT

Into Your Bathroom

Have you looked at the toilet paper in a store? There are a lot of choices! You can buy big rolls with extra sheets. You can buy one-ply, two-ply, or even three-ply toilet paper. These rolls have more than one layer of paper on the roll. The layers stick together and make the paper thick. You can also buy recycled toilet paper. It helps save trees!

In the bathroom, take a look at the toilet paper roll. Do you see a pattern? Touch it. Is it soft? Try to see if

Most Americans use 384 trees worth of toilet paper over their lives.

it is made from recycled paper or not. You may have never noticed the roll before. But a lot of work went into every roll!

There are many kinds of toilet paper you can buy.

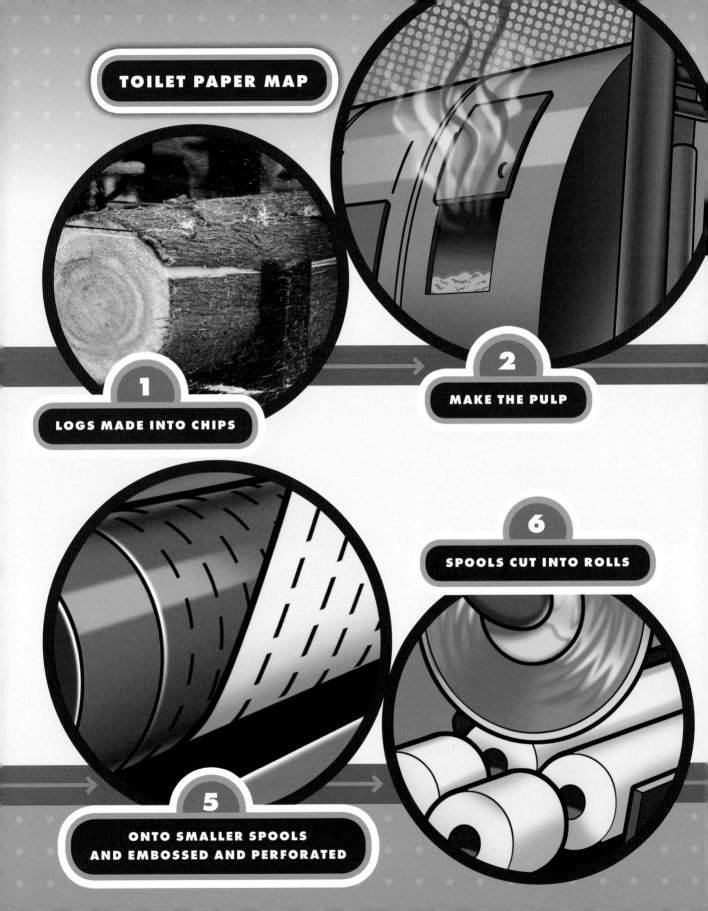

TOILET PAPER MAP

1 LOGS MADE INTO CHIPS

2 MAKE THE PULP

6 SPOOLS CUT INTO ROLLS

5 ONTO SMALLER SPOOLS AND EMBOSSED AND PERFORATED

3

PULP SPREAD ON SCREENS

4

ONTO A GIANT SPOOL

8

TO THE STORE

7

ROLLS WRAPPED

GLOSSARY

absorb (ab-ZORB): To absorb is to soak up a liquid. Pulp has to be dry to absorb chemicals.

bleached (BLEECHD): Something is bleached when it is made whiter or cleaner. Pulp is bleached to make white toilet paper.

chemicals (KEM-uh-kuhlz): Chemicals are substances made using chemistry. Chemicals are used to bleach pulp.

conveyor belt (kuhn-VAY-ur BELT): A conveyor belt is a moving belt that takes materials from one place to another in a factory. Toilet paper rolls move to different machines on a conveyor belt.

crepe (KRAPE): To crepe paper is to make it have wrinkles. Metal blades crepe the toilet paper.

embossed (em-BOSSD): Embossed paper has a design or pattern pressed into it. Most toilet paper is embossed.

evaporates (i-VAP-uh-rates): A liquid evaporates when it turns into a gas. Water evaporates from the wood chips when they are heated.

fiber (FY-bur): Fiber is a thread that forms in parts of certain plants, such as cotton. There is fiber in wood.

filter (FIL-tur): A filter has many holes that let small pieces fall through it while holding larger pieces. The pulp from recycled paper goes through a filter.

lignin (LIG-nin): Lignin is a kind of natural glue in trees that keeps wood fibers together. To make paper, lignin is taken out from pulp.

perforated (PUR-fuh-rayt-id): Something becomes perforated when it has a row of small holes through it. Each roll of toilet paper is perforated.

pulp (PUHLP): Pulp is the soft, juicy flesh parts of fruit or a soft, wet mixture. Wood pulp becomes paper.

renewable (ri-NOO-uh-bul): Something is renewable if when it is used or old it can be replaced with something new. Trees are renewable.

BOOKS

Bocker, Susan. *Paper Trail*. New York: Children's Press, 2007.

Snyder, Inez. *Trees to Paper*. New York: Rosen, 2003.

Woods, Samuel G. *Made in the USA—Recycled Paper*. Farmington Hills, MI: Blackbirch Press, 2000.

INDEX

Visit our Web site for links about toilet paper production: childsworld.com/links

Note to Parents, Teachers, and Librarians: We routinely verify our Web links to make sure they are safe and active sites. So encourage your readers to check them out!